I'VE GOT YOUR NUMBER!

THE INSIDER'S GUIDE: ONE WOMAN'S PRIVATE
SECRETS TO SALES AND SALES MANAGEMENT

Lana Cloud, GRI, CRB, President and Broker,
Kache Realty Group, LLC

ISBN 978-0-557-16570-4

Introduction

Over the years, I've learned many things that can shorten a new manager's learning curve and assist in understanding the unwritten rules for us—women—in leadership positions. For example, find out before a meeting what the agenda is to include are so you can discuss them intelligently. Most firms will furnish an agenda ahead of time for this purpose. If they aren't in the habit of doing so, it's not a well organized firm. Also, sit in a power position during meetings. The second power position at a rectangular conference table is to the right hand of the leader. If you get there early, you can get this seat. Get it three or more times, and the team will assume you have become one of the ranking players. First, make sure no one regularly sits there, such as the CFO or the marketing director. If someone does, the third best place is at the other end of the table. The fourth best place is the seat immediately to the left of the leader.

I will also share some management or leadership mistakes that firms make, which will clue you in whether or not the firm you're affiliated with is a safe bet for your future career. The responsibility of leadership in any sales business is to help sales people learn how to produce faster, easier, and more effectively. Since the Internet is a proven source of business for sales professionals, I have focused on lead-generating systems, time management, business planning, and marketing plans you can use anywhere, especially if you want to go into business for yourself.

Lastly, there are some great stories about my experiences, and I hope you get a chuckle over them.

I remember my very first strategic planning event as a brand new manager. A three-day meeting was held outside of corporate so that we could all focus on delivering a valid projection of the next six month's office production. All us managers—thirteen men and three women—were supposed to bring their budget plans, but since I was just hired, I had no idea what to submit or how it was to be prepared. My SVP, my boss, assured me he "had it covered for me." The CEO was a sort of no-nonsense kind of guy and went around to each manager asking for their projected numbers. I was so afraid of making a bad impression, afraid that the SVP would give out incorrect numbers, afraid of being embarrassed, and afraid of not knowing what I should say, that I hyperventilated and passed out cold in the adjacent hallway while trying to escape to the lady's room for a brief getting-it-together respite. Well, I definitely did make an impression on all present. Frankly, I think they were all rather amused that I was so nervous that I fainted, and they cut me some slack for the next two days. It was the only time in my career I ever went into a budget meeting not fully prepared. I did hyperventilate a few times, but with knowledge, I outgrew it.

And there was the time, I held my very first open house in the windy New Mexico summer. As I placed the sign outside, the wind blew the door shut, and I had to climb through the bathroom window to get back in. By the time I made it back in, I was hot, tired, thirsty, dirty, and a little worse for the wear. Thank goodness no one came to the open house. I always wondered if anyone had seen me squeezing my size 8 body through that size 2 window.

There was also the time I was previewing homes for an upper-end buyer, and the house was supposed to be vacant. In an upstairs bath, I found a warm curling iron and personal items; I also found a room with clothes piled on the floor. The hair stood up on the back of my neck. I never found anyone in the house, and neither did the listing broker who came out and searched. However, the next time I previewed homes, I took another agent with me. And, of course, there are management anecdotes, too, coming up later in this book.

The Good Old Boy versus the Good Old Girl

I guess it's a good thing that I was an only child and my father treated me like one of the guys. My mom was a very beautiful, generous, and loving parent, and she taught me all about makeup, style, and effective communication. But when I was growing up, I watched boxing matches, golf matches, tennis matches, and baseball and football games. I went hunting and skinned, fried, and ate squirrel and other game. I played baseball, badminton, tennis, and volleyball; I fenced, bowled, and even played a little bit of football. There were even times when Dad let me help work on our family car and others he had secured at a cheap price. Of course, those were the days before the automobile industry had come up with fuel-injected engines. I have to tell you that these "male" bonding experiences and learned habits prepared me well for having success in a man's world. For example, have you ever noticed how many business terms are relative to "guy" sports?

It was a "slam-dunk."

Let's tee it up and see how it goes:

That hit the mark.

Let's kick it around the bases and see if we can hit a home run.

Let's cover all the bases.

Why don't we go for a home run? We could hit it out of the park!

Let's run it up the flagpole.

Don't worry, it will run its course.

Well hell, let's just punt.

We weren't able to get first base on that one.

He didn't get to first base!

I think you get the idea. Male children and men engage in team sports and sports activities from the time they learn to walk. If they happen to not be athletic, they still follow the teams, attend games, and know about the sporting world. So we, as career women—as career people—have to learn the sport vernacular that goes along with becoming a professional in a man's world. When you do, it becomes much easier to win at the business game. It sure worked well for me, even though it may have been an accident in the beginning. Most of my mentors were men who treated me as an equal, but I can't say that usually happens for most women. I credit my success to the fact I learned at an early age to *think like one of the guys*—specifically, I learned the team mentality. I found that male bonding and becoming an insider revolved around many sporting events and/or activities. For example, coming into a meeting before it starts, you'll usually find "the guys" talking about what sporting events they attended the previous weekend, which teams are vying for what, and when the next golf outing is coming. Being able to discuss teams or play golf is an advantage toward getting accepted as one of the guys. If the leaders are women, you have the same task: find, learn, and use what things interest them in their organization.

If you didn't grow up with the same kind of background as your co-workers, you can learn, and I can help you by directing you to a few books that describe how leaders think in the business world. (1)

Another important aspect in being accepted relates to education. Degrees matter in business today, especially in the top echelons. If you don't have an MBA, then obtain some training that is credible and has a reputation. For example, I went to Georgetown University and obtained a master's degree in information technology management. The program took about a year and a half weekends and nights, and I learned all about Internet marketing. It has served me well when I needed credentials that impress. Here's another example: if you are in finance, an MBA from Wharton or Harvard would be impressive. However, it is helpful to research a firm to find out where the major players attained their degrees. You'll often find that many of them are alumni from the same universities.

For over thirty years, my field has been real estate sales and management. I got every kind of management training offered by every company that I affiliated with. I even went to school to become a professional trainer for real estate certifiable programs. We had to develop scenarios that could be done in twenty minutes or less. Having to prepare full presentations within a limited time frame taught me to think quickly with logic and intelligence. This will serve you well also because you'll find that men are often impressed by speed versus content: meetings are for addressing the issues and discussing that issue or the items on the agenda. The best way to get insider information is to listen to discussions during lunch, at coffee breaks, or before meetings. Information or facts you share should be on point, clearly stated, and brief. To achieve this, always endeavor to learn what the agenda is for the upcoming meeting: research the issues and have the pertinent information—don't assume or guess. If you find the discussion centering around a topic you didn't anticipate, listen and take notes so you can find out why this topic is on the agenda unexpectedly.

Remember that, as in most cases, perception is everything. In meetings, most leaders don't like chitchat or establishing rapport—that was done prior to beginning the meeting. They like to get at the heart of the matter, address the issues, and move on. For god's sakes- they want to get out on the golf course as soon as possible. It's best to be quiet, thoughtful, and attentive if you don't have anything to share. If you jump in and don't hit the mark, you will get blank stares, sudden awkward silences, a clearing of the throat, and someone else's input forthcoming. If you continue to have these off-the-mark comments, you'll find yourself excluded from upcoming meetings. Be observant, you'll see what gets heard and what input has merit. You can great information by observing body language: folded arms, scooting back from the table, leaning back in a chair, are signs of disagreement or concern. Leaning forward, elbows on table, sitting on the edge of a seat, are signs of interest and commitment.

From my own personal history and experiences, I find that most men and their activities with their families, around their families, on vacation, and after work are related to sports. I have been married to my current husband for twenty years. He is the perfect example of a sports-based existence. He was a superjock in basketball back in the '60s. It was and is the highlight of his life. He even still has his good old boy network fully intact after forty years has passed. They still get together regularly and discuss the same history, year after year, event after event, and relive the good old days.

So as a woman or young lady looking for a career niche, it is helpful to analyze just who you're talking to. Once a person has spent a lifetime playing and relating to sports, this love of team will continue. Knowing this, become informed about sports, learn current sports statistics and rankings of football and basketball teams. Basketball has March Madness and football has the Super Bowl; tennis has the US Open and Wimbledon. Golf has the Masters in April every year. You gotta watch and learn. This will create *immediate approval,* particularly if you play golf and also have a handicap under 30.

I became one of five general partners of a large firm in 1989, and of the five, three were excellent golfers. They arranged play whenever we had go-away meetings, and of course, they talked business as they played After a few months, I realized that I was missing out on these general partner moments of value. I was in my late forties at the time, not usually when you take on a new sport like golf, but it was important that I be on the course with them. So I asked them if they would instruct me, and I could play along with them. Lucky for me, they were all for me, and I learned to play golf. I still play today and enjoy it very much. Would it have been easier just to ignore the truth and let them go out together? Of course. But, I wanted to be a big player in a big pond, so I did what I had to do and really enjoyed doing it.

It made a difference in my status within the team, and it brought me closer to the CEO, who turned out to be my most important mentor of all. Most of these men have wives who are not into participative sports because they're into aerobic exercise or jogging or even a little tennis. They don't usually play in the same circle as their husbands. The CEOs, COOs, and VPs are usually of the same background, at least in terms of career, and in the same age group. Of course, their preference is generally family first, then friends. If they have cohorts in need, then they make sure to arrange that help. Us good old girls are left in the dust. But there are some rules that can put us on equal ground:

One: Obtain as much education as you can. It can be job specific, but if it's not also worthy (coming from the supported educational institutions), the salary may not be equal. A top-notch education can get you a good entry level position and even further along in the good old boy's network. If your degree is from the University of Texas, you might want to spend a summer at Harvard, Yale, Stanford, or Princeton in some classes relative to the industry in which you wish to excel.

Two: Learn all you can about baseball, basketball, football, and hockey. Horse racing and boxing are also helpful. *Golf is a must,* and you should learn to play as soon as possible. The two sports you might play would be golf and tennis, but I can't tell you how many important corporate decisions were, and are, made on the golf course. You have to be there or you can't play. So sign up for golf lessons. An understanding mentor or other women or savvy younger guys may even teach you. You get credit for trying and for being persistent and part of the team.

Three: There is an incalculable focus placed on the word and concept team. It's sort of like the Three Musketeers: One for all, and all for one. But if you're not the old line member with a history, then you may find yourself not part of the insider team. There's a realistic truth that goes along with this, and that is the fact that if you are never allowed inside, you can never achieve your career goals—you'll never have a chance to even go there. In addressing the team concept, and in addressing top women leaders in an organization, one must figure out for one's self what the personal dynamic is within the firm. I am also assuming that you know competence always counts. All things being equal, female counterparts are as competent as males.

Maybe this is an erroneous assumption, but competence and ability certainly are at the top of the list in terms of success and career advancement. The things discussed herein about women gaining an edge in a man's business world are tools to make it go smoother and faster. Learn to play golf reasonably well. Be able to tee it up, hit the ball, and get moving. Whiffing (missing) the ball does not engender positive impressions. Being able to keep up with the pace of play is also important. If you hit the ball six times and you are not in the cup, pick up the ball. Experienced golfers don't want to wait around while you hit the ball ten times. Learn the etiquette of golf: count your strokes accurately, never talk or move when someone is teeing up and starts to drive. Rake any trap you find yourself in; even though it is hard work, and may be hot work, it is necessary. If you take a divot out of the fairway, find it and replace it. If you look for your lost ball five minutes, that's long enough. Take a penalty stroke, drop a new ball, and hit it. And, never, never cheat on your score. Golf is one of those sports suffused with honor and integrity. Knowing these rules of etiquette, as well as making a genuine effort to learn the game, will earn you kudos.

Four: Learn how to cuss authoritatively if you find it appropriate in your business environment. It takes practice. You cannot say the "f," "c," or "mf" words. That's too far over the acceptable limits. Women have made great strides in business over the past twenty years, and we can *usually* have the freedom of our male counterparts. However, women using some curse words will not be found palatable by many business associates—male as well as female. There is such inelegance about certain words even if society has embraced them. Using them at a business meeting or at a black tie function somehow reduces a person to a lesser status. Men do have more tolerance for each other using foul language. It may be prejudicial, but still, use of some curse words will create the perception that the woman is harsh, crass, and hard. I think the fact is that most people don't really like hearing curse words at all, either from men or women, but since women are female and being female is identified with femininity, cursing or expletives is the antithesis, and just hit's the wrong note. You can say the usual, and men can say the "f" word, but the other two are off limits to them, too! If they use those words, you want to work somewhere else.

Five: Wear comfortable and stylish business casual attire. Check out what the veterans around the firm wear. If you don't know how to put it together, go to a professional, and let them show you. You do not want to look like a slut going into the office. It may get you noticed, but you won't get any respect. For example, a V-neck shirt showing deep cleavage should not be worn to work. Shiny fabrics such as satin, lamé, and taffeta are not proper attire for an office. Silk is very nice choice. A nice dress with a jacket, pants with a matching top and a jacket, or two coordinated pieces of compatible colors are good. If you can't sit down and button your pants or straighten your skirt, it is too tight. Butts should not be cupped by the fabric. Pockets should be at the hip line and not stand open, and buttons should not be missing or pinned on. Shoes should not flop or clack against the floor and should be polished and clean. High heels are OK as long as you can walk in them easily.

Let's talk about nails and hair. Nails should be done: unpolished or polished, it doesn't matter, but they need to look good and modern, not like spotted claws. Wild, crazy jewelry of large size should be avoided. I was always into pins of matching coordination. I never liked dangly jewelry, but times have changed, and more people do wear the dangly earrings. They should just not be gaudy or too large. Hair should be cut, shaped, dyed, or whatever is best to look good. . And, of course, hair should be clean and shiny. There's nothing worse than seeing a nice-looking professional with two-inch dark, grey, or white roots showing against the scalp.

There is also hosiery and undergarments. Most women in the Southwest do not wear hosiery as it is simply too hot. On the other hand, most legs there are tan, so it's not too bad. Hairy legs in any climate should be taken care of. I, myself, hate to wear panty hose, but I will when it's appropriate and necessary to be professional. Everyone should wear sufficient supportive undergarments that allow for modesty and coverage. I always prefer slips that have the bra built in, so it is one piece, comfortable, and modest.

Each firm has its own customs and preferences, and by observation, a newcomer can see what kind of standard has been established. Most firms have gone to business casual, but this is not so in the Northeast, like Boston, New York, and Philadelphia. Most businesspersons there still dress in white shirts, suits, and ties. Women generally wear suits, blouses, and high heels as well as hose and bras.

Hot Tips on Career Advancement for Women & Men

One: Stay the hell away from family-owned businesses if you want a long term career. You can have the best skills known to mankind and you still won't get ahead, especially if the man has children or relatives because they will always fall heir to the business—even if they are incompetent or lazy.

Two: Never fool around or become intimate with an office business associate, especially someone who is your boss or your boss's boss. This is a no-brainer and a no-win. Just don't do it.

Three: Be proactive. Create, innovate, think! Come up with inventive solutions. Take the risk; it'll be worth it. Go directly to the person in charge of implementing your idea or solution rather than to your immediate boss. I know, usually this is not acceptable; however, you will find if it's a good idea and you don't go directly, he'll get credit for it, and you'll never even get mentioned. This is really a judgment call from you. You should determine just what kind of character your supervisor or boss has, but one can be fooled. I always just took it for granted that my boss was out for him or herself.

Four: Be on time, alert, and ready for anything. Stay late if needed. Never appear to be a clock watcher.

Five: Be neat and clean and well-groomed. Have nice breath, clean teeth, and a nice smile. Have clean, groomed, and clean, manicured nails. Don't do your hair or nails at work or in meetings. And don't chew gum; it's annoying and not cool.

Six: Don't whine! Don't complain at work to anyone; don't complain about staff, your boss, or anyone's boss. Do not talk rumors or scandals. Keep confidences. Call your mom if you need to vent: she always understands!

Seven: I don't recommend working when you're ill, but you do need to be careful about taking too many days off for doctor appointments or female issues. Dependability in career goals is paramount and if you are away too much, upper management's perception is that you cannot be counted on to be there when they need you. Your personal health arrangements should never be obvious.

Eight: Quiet listening is most often perceived as wisdom, so don't chat incessantly or loudly. Listen and watch what everyone else does— body language, eye contact. Be an observer.

Common Mistakes Leaders Make

It is very tough to bring a business to profit and lead its members through an uncertain economy and unpredictable markets. When leaders fail to adhere to established leadership tenets, employees or, in some cases, independent contractors either jump ship, stay on board, or flounder and perform at reduced levels. There are typical mistakes that leaders, corporations, firms, and organizations typically make. If you are working with a firm that commits the mistakes listed here, you should consider searching for new employment. If you are interviewing with a firm, you should know what to look for:

1. Failure to create a vision and communicate it effectively to all involved. It is absolutely essential that the leader and his or her team share the goals and company vision so all employees or independent sales people realize what the game plan is. The employees or agents want to know where the organization is going and how that will impact them. The more the leader shares the plan and vision, the more trust and leadership he or she will establish. If you are interviewing with a firm, all the top people and managers should know the vision of the company. If there is vagueness and they all explain it differently, it could mean they don't have it together.

2. Unclear expectations. This is a result of failing to create a vision and communicating it effectively. Leaders, when they know where the firm is going, should know what each division needs to accomplish. These expectations will be qualified and clearly communicated to each management and other member. Undoubtedly, as circumstances, finances, objectives, and directions change, the leader will need to update team members.

3. Lack of trust. This is a result of mistakes one and two. When you tell people what's going to happen and then it does, they learn to have faith in your decision making and in your clarity of communication. When employees or sales people don't have that faith, they will look for someone else, either inside or outside the organization, to follow. Trust is based on having honesty and integrity. It's all about keeping promises, being fair, and being visible to all of the sales force. Leaders of any company will be judged by what they do every day. Once you lose the trust of your staff, your employees, and your independent contractors, it is extremely difficult to reestablish it. Quite often it can never be recovered until a new leader comes in and delivers the vision and a new strategic plan.

4. Setting a poor behavioral example. As the leader of the company, the leader must demonstrate those behaviors desired in others. When you become a leader, you don't have the right to blame someone else or let your own performance suffer. There is no break time for a leader—he or she is always onstage, and people are always watching to see how they handle things: making decisions, answering tough questions, and communicating. If you talk the talk, you must walk the walk!

For example, I remember a case where the leader of our company was very adamant about his vision and the future of the company. It sounded very good! Unfortunately, rarely did the employees or independent contractors ever see him in one of the branches. The employees and independent contractors never knew for sure what was going on with upper-level management or how the firm was exactly doing in the tough economic times. Many other real estate firms were merging with others or going into bankruptcy, so naturally there was concern for us, too. No one had discussed the economic situation with the middle-management team either, so communication regarding the status of the firm was nonexistent. Plus "someone" kept changing the programs and systems all the time, and the services touted to the sales people never materialized. There was no explanation for the changes, and the managers of the branches—the leaders of the branch offices—began to be removed as a cost-cutting measure. And, since the agents depended on these communications to keep informed, no one knew for sure what the heck was going on, and this created an environment of insecurity and lack of trust—the real killer of any business. Ref 2

5. Failure to retain experienced and competent employees. Often, when there is a breakdown in communication, middle-management gets mixed signals from the leader at the top. When office managers become uncertain as to the future stability of the company, they lose trust in the leader, which is bound to be perceived not only by the employees, but also by the sales people.

When middle management loses trust in the leadership, top producers—the talent, the ones who actually generate the firm's income—tend to depart. The managers themselves are at a loss to know exactly what their position is so they are forced to make assumptions that may be totally off the mark. So not only is the firm losing the sales agent talent, but it's also losing the manager talent.

6. Input from the wrong people. Sometimes, upper management or the leader listens only to those close to them, becoming isolated and insulated from the truth as it exists out in the field. If a leader doesn't take the time and the effort to personally and talk with the troops, he or she will not know what they are thinking, what they are worried about, and what they want and need. A leader has to be involved enough to know what truth is out there. It may not be what he or she heard from the insular staff at headquarters. It could be entirely different from what is perceived at the highest levels. Leaders need to *know* what the real truth is.

7. Failure to follow through. If the leadership plans some program, creates a contest, or develops a new training program—and everyone has agreed to it—it needs to happen. It shouldn't just disappear because it wasn't delegated properly. Responsibility is inherent in following through. Ref 6,8

8. Failure to use outside talent and resources. If cost cutting has had an impact on providing services to the agents, it is certainly acceptable to use outside resources such as speakers, motivators, marketing, and training. Some will volunteer to share their knowledge if asked. Plus, there is always a ton of in-house talent to be accessed as resources if they are only asked. I used to use the agents in the office as trainers in their various areas of expertise. Not only did it give them a valuable positive attitude, but also it allowed the agents to learn from their peers.

9. Underestimating needed financial resources. Most businesses fail within the first couple of years because the owners and/or partners didn't allow for the true costs of running the firm. One must project not only the best case scenario, but also the worst case and have a game plan for both that will work. If future funds may be needed, they should be planned for up front, committed to, and saved or invested to earn interest until the time they are needed. Anticipating the challenges is the job of a smart leader. Signs that the planning wasn't sufficient may be observed by the lack of employee staffing, lack of supplies, a loss of agents, and managers running multiple branches. Ref 8

10. Insufficient recognition of sales staff and/or managers. Even if it is just one percent growth, everyone should be recognized for successes and congratulated. Sales associates or employees should get handwritten notes from the owner when they accomplish a personal milestone or get recognized by their peer group. Appreciation goes a long way toward building trust and loyalty. It should be a mutual admiration society.

11. Failure to handle criticism, suggestions, or concerns from staff or agents in a positive, proactive manner. When leadership asks for input and creative ideas from middle management then demeans, ignores, or criticizes that input, then a "fear" society is created, which is extremely negative for building a healthy management team. It is even worse if the leadership communicates in the parent-child mode, which is when adults are talked down to as if they are small children needing guidance, advice, and direction. It is disrespectful and discouraging.

12. Sharing negativity or saying too much. When times are tough, funding is touchy, concerns are paramount, and profits are negligible, a proactive, results-oriented plan should be what is shared with the business family. No team needs to hear over and over that if something doesn't happen to fix it, they are all dead meat. Saying this to the management team is a sure way to create fear, depression, and doubts. It is also not a healthy way to inspire, especially when the issue of performance is involved. Getting everyone involved in—and committed to— the solutions is a positive way to solve even severe issues and give hope and a sense of empowerment. Dumping on middle management is not productive. Telling them what they must do is not enough, and it implies success or failure is on their heads alone. It's like telling a student he or she must learn calculus in three weeks or his or her family will be exiled. Teaching the student calculus, with specific goals and measurement, is the productive way to get the desired results. Telling just doesn't get much done.

13. Spending money on items perceived as unnecessary in tough times. When leadership has focused on budgetary items, cost-cutting events, and downsizing issues, then turns around and holds a picnic or a party, it sends mixed signals and does not engender trust. It is perceived by the troops as ineffective and insensitive when they believe they have sacrificed their needs for the company.

Focus and Your Positive Self-image

It's hard for us to always maintain a positive self-image. Real estate and other sales professionals tend to have highs and lows when it comes to self-image. It depends on how well the business is going and the cash flow coming in. If it's busy—clients are happy, sales are happening, homes are selling—then we all tend to be happy with ourselves and have a positive, ego-driven self-image. Unfortunately, we don't always have highs. To prevent lows from happening often, there are a few concrete steps that can create a level of discipline that will help.

STEP ONE: Decide what it is you really want. This is very important because without knowing what you really want, you will have difficulty envisioning it. Without a vision, you limit yourself greatly. Having a clear vision is inspirational and gives you confidence in your abilities and your plan to succeed no matter what the environment delivers. And the great thing is you can have more than one vision.

STEP TWO: Determine the activities that will lead to your chosen goal. This means listing all the things you, or your team, can do for the results to happen. There are many different paths to reach an outcome. I suggest avoiding activities that don't fit your personality. Choose ones you feel comfortable with and that will ensure your goal. For example, if you are not comfortable working with for sale by owners, don't make it part of your plan. You won't get around to doing it because you don't really want to. But, if you like working with expired listings, showing sellers where improvements can be made, does it. It will give you confidence and enjoyment doing something you find rewarding and satisfying.

STEP THREE: Spend twenty minutes a day thinking about what you want to achieve—this is focused quiet time where you revisit your goals. See them; picture what will happen and how you will feel when you get your desired results. Focus on your goals first thing in the morning and sometime after dinner in the evening.

Choose times when you know you will have peace and quiet.

Concentration and thinking often happen when you're taking a shower, sitting in the tub, weeding the garden, vacuuming, or doing mundane things that allow your mind to wander and conceive. This includes the time during your commute home. Have you ever been driving along and noticed you have no clue where you are? Your mind was somewhere else entirely—this is focused time. So train yourself to use it wisely and focus your mind on seeing your vision and results.

People who get continual results typically believe in their abilities and in the law of abundance and the law of attraction. These proven theories believe that we can have whatever we want in life by creating a conscious connection to the greater universe and having it contribute toward the desired results. A positive self-image is created by picturing or envisioning already having the results you want. Sharing these goals with a group you trust, can bring support, encouragement, and self confidence in your abilities. Ref 1, 5

How to Keep your Mojo Alive

Support groups

You simply cannot survive in today's fast-paced, ever-changing global economy without the support of like-minded individuals who are open to sharing and committed to success, growth, and learning to assist you along the way. The right group can provide the fundamental resources for building your business. Professional groups can be made up from a group of peers in the exact same industry, a group of companies that focus on the same vertical market or market segment, or just a group of business leaders that are ready to help out those just starting out. The right professional group can be a conduit to growth and success within your small business.

But what should you look for? Here are some guidelines to assist you in creating or finding the right group.

1. **Shared Vision**. It is critically important that your group have a shared vision. You need to make sure that everyone is on the same wavelength and committed to the vision of the group. As you observe and listen to the participants, you will discover what you have in common and if your goals relate to theirs. If your goals don't match, seek out a different group.

2. **Trust**. Trust is a major factor in the success of any business group. You must be able to trust that issues, challenges, and needs are kept confidential within the group. When you have complete trust with your group, it is amazing how you and your colleagues open up and share challenges, pains, frustrations, and weaknesses with each other.

3. **Teamwork**. Creating the right team is important to the success of any professional group. When you have a team of like-minded professionals assembled for one common goal or shared vision, the results can be extraordinary. Your peers in your group will be on the lookout for opportunities to help you and your business grow, and you will be doing the same for them. Besides sharing business opportunities,

there are a number of different areas that sharing starts to happen, these can range from business to personal dreams, goals, challenges, and issues. The team is there to help you succeed.

4. **Open Mind and Heart**. Successful groups keep an open mind and also an open heart with others in the group. No one person can do it alone, and the support of the team is critical to its success. If you are the type of person that can open your mind to new ideas and open your heart to building new, strong relationships, then your professional group will be an overwhelming success. Be open and honest, let your guard down, and be willing to share with others. Remember to give from the heart: in the long run, givers always receive more than what they give.

5. **Commitment**. This is, perhaps, the most important key to success. Groups that have committed members will have endless opportunities. Members need to be committed to getting their goals accomplished on time, committed to sharing their resources and learning, committed to helping each member grow his or her business, committed to the group in general. When you have a room of committed members, your group becomes a trusted, well oiled forum for dynamic ideas and it becomes an extension of your family

6. **Fun**. This is the most important tip. If you are not having fun doing what you are doing, why are you doing it? If you are the business owner, do not force your employees to attend training or a function that is beneath their level of experience. Sell them on the importance of the concept and then let them choose if they want to attend. However, fun is one of the critical components to a successful group. Have fun, learn, open up, and give of yourself.

7. **Respect for Other Members'** Time. Be on time when attending your professional group. Nothing shows more disrespect to others than consistently showing up late. Also, don't monopolize the group's time by speaking too much. It is important to listen to others and allow everyone to have an equal opportunity to speak.

8. **Growth**. One of the most important tips that I have found is to step out of your comfort zone when participating in your group. These groups are hard work; there is no coasting when you are working effectively, there will be growth experiences that challenge your mind and make you examine who you are and what your company stands for. Be ready to work hard and challenge yourself. You will start to reap the benefits associated with a successful professional group. Ref 5,6

Time Management

Yes, I know you've heard it before, but it is important!

The Benefits of Time Management

Who will benefit from developing effective time management?

- Everyone. Anyone who needs to get results, increase productivity, spend more time with family, multitask, and gain control over his or her personal and business life.

You need to develop effective time management if you say to yourself

- I don't always feel in control
- I need to increase my productivity
- I have to juggle a multitude of tasks
- I'm always being interrupted
- I'd love to have more time for the things I enjoy but never get the time

Basics of Time Management

You will be able to:

- Manage priorities
- Plan your essential priorities. What comes first: is it business, family, religion, self improvement? When you have figured this out, you can begin to delegate your time accordingly.
- Increase work effectiveness and productivity
- Enjoy a more balanced lifestyle
- Feel more in control of your daily activities
- Reduce the stress that results from a lack of effective time planning
- Prioritize and schedule tasks

Delegation

If there's a job you don't enjoy—administrative or otherwise—try to get someone else to do it. I used to have my kids organize my house tours for me. They were good at it. All I had to do was pick up their lists, and I was on my way.

Developing a personal sense of time

People who are always late, or never get finished with a project often underestimate the task and the time it will take to get it done properly. When you are tracking and organizing your time, hour by hour, you will discover just where you are underestimating time needed for the job.

Identifying long-term goals

All the activities you engage in on a daily basis should be supportive of and contributory to your long-term objectives. If your activities don't do that, reexamine them.

Making middle and long-term plans

Creating and implementing these action plans are very specific to the individual, but they should be written, in detail, with dates, and focused on daily. Be sure you know what you are asking for; you will probably get it via the plan you generate.

Managing paperwork

There's your paperwork and the paperwork you are required to give to someone else. Paying bills is something that has to happen, but it can be done faster and more efficiently online. Plus, you get annual records you can use for taxes.

Organizing your office and your workstation

It's as simple as having a place for everything and keeping it consistent.

Time stealers

In order for a time management process to work, it is important to know what aspects of your personal management need to be improved. Below you will find some of the most frequent reasons for reduced effectiveness in the workplace. Note the ones that are major obstacles to your own time management.

1. Telephone Interruptions

Have you ever had one of those days when you thought your true calling was in telemarketing? The telephone—the greatest communication tool—can be your biggest enemy if you don't know how to control its hold over you. Try to fix definite times when you would not like to be disturbed, and make the system work except for genuine emergencies. If you have several phone calls to make, do them all in a burst.

2. Drop-in Visitors

The five deadliest words that rob your time are "Have you got a minute." Everyone's the culprit: colleagues, the boss. Knowing how to deal with interruptions is one of the best skills you can learn. Ask people who come to you with problems to propose their own solutions. Throw that monkey right back on their shoulders so they'll grow to meet their own challenges.

3. Meetings

Unfortunately, managers are expected to attend many meetings—organizational, training, office, educational. The most helpful thing is to get these schedules as far out as possible, record them in your calendar, and build the rest of your time around them.

4. Ineffective Delegation

Good delegation is considered a key skill in both managers and leaders. The best managers have an ability to delegate work to staff and ensure it is done correctly. This is probably the best way of building a team's morale and reducing your workload at the same time. The general rule is if one of your staff can do it 80 percent as well as you can, and then delegate it.

5. Procrastination and Indecision

The biggest thief of time is not decision making but decision avoidance. By reducing your amount of procrastination, you can substantially increase the amount of active time available to you. Do not postpone important matters that are unpleasant. Jobs rarely get more pleasant by being postponed. Do them first thing every morning, and the rest of your day will be more productive

6. Lack of Priorities/Objectives

This is probably the biggest, cause of totally wasted time it affects all we do both professionally and personally. Those who accomplish the most in a day know exactly what they want to accomplish. Unfortunately, too many of us think that goals and objectives are yearly things and not daily considerations. These results in too much time spent on the minor things and not on the things that are important to our work and lives having a prioritized plan of action for each day allows for effective time management.

7. Acting on Incomplete Information

You can spend hours working on a solution only to find out that the agent, whether out of fear or retribution, failed to give you complete information. It's important for a manager to ask the right questions in order to solve a problem. Learn to make a list of questions whose answers you'll need to solve the problem. Once you understand the problem, then you can solve it.

8. Dealing with Team Members

Plan scheduled time for discussing routine matters with your colleagues or staff. Then you will avoid interrupting each other all the time. The time spent with them should be rewarding and focused on their needs. You'll get a lot done when you allow your team the time they need to air their thoughts, make suggestions, and just have some fun.

9. Crisis Management (Fire Fighting)

The best way to handle these kinds of interruptions is by setting aside one to two hours each day just in case crises come up. As the manager, you will generally know how your team works—morning people, night people—and build your safety hours around that. Crises can be business related or even personal, but it still takes time to deal with them. First, find out the facts. Knowing them will let you know if you, personally, have to handle the emergency or if someone, namely the agent involved, can do it with direction and delegation. I believe that agents should learn to handle most of their transaction emergencies unless a broker's credentials and authority is needed. Agents have to be taught how to do it, but once taught, they are capable of solving most of their own problems.

10. Unclear Communication

Often, time is used up doing the wrong task when you think you are doing the right one. Be sure if you plan on following up on a task assigned to you that you not only know what the specific task is, but also make sure you are the right person to do it.

11. Inadequate Technical Knowledge

This can be a very big and frustrating time waster. If you are not an expert on the computer or have difficulty using Excel, Publisher, or other programs, either learn the systems or find someone else to do it for you. I have seen both managers and agents spend hours fooling around, trying to figure out how to make a brochure or a flyer or write a formal letter. This is not the best use of their time. As a manager, if you are not proficient, you must go to a class and learn so you don't spend hours trying to learn on your own, or you must have an administrative person to whom you can delegate these tasks. Otherwise, you will drive yourself crazy

12. Lack of Planning

Not only make daily and monthly lists of things that have to be done, but also make sure you keep the completed lists and analyze them closely. Arrange routine times for jobs such as going through the mail, talking with your manager or staff, computer input, and so on.

13. Stress and Fatigue

Many people today feel that they have to accomplish everything yesterday, so they don't give themselves enough time to do things properly. This leads to half-finished projects and no feelings of achievement. Learn to say no. Get used to asking yourself, "Am I the right person for this job?" Before answering yes, ask yourself if you really want to or should get involved.

14. Personal Disorganization

It's simple: You should have a list of what you plan on accomplishing each day. Allocate time for each task as well as tasks you do not have direct control over such as meetings and emergencies. Your desk should be clean, organized, and uncluttered. You should return calls according to your time plan, not those calling you. Go through mail, handle it once, and assign tasks to be done then or later. Finish each task or allocate a time for it, and move on. Completion of tasks is one key to personal time organizational success. Ref 6,8

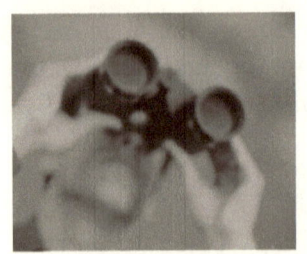

Business Planning

Any primer would be incomplete without talking about goal setting and business planning. Every achiever of any renown has created a business plan. It can be simply a list of what you want for yourself in life, or it could be as complex as a grad thesis. What matters is that you, personally, decide what your goals are and organize a plan to get them. Later in this chapter you will find a very simple form for you to write down your goals in detail. This process is important! Writing down and thinking about each goal and each objective is important.

Duplicate this page for each objective and get specific—each objective should have a target date for completion. The objective should be reasonable and attainable within the time limit you choose. You can have as many objectives as you want, but you *must write them down in detail.*

Earlier we discussed the importance of quiet, focused time. One method of finding this is the newest facilitation in helping people achieve their desired goals—the focus video. These videos can be purchased, or you can create your own through PowerPoint or video. In each frame, an objective is stated in the present tense. For example, "I have all the money I need." This is accompanied by a picture or video illustrating the statement. The next frame says, "I deserve the finest things in life," which is again accompanied by pictures of what that means to you. It may be a mansion, a fine car, or a vacation home. You choose, but the process of composing this PowerPoint or video accesses your subconscious mind, allowing it to work on the desired results without your consciously thinking about it. However, if you watch the video or review your written objectives daily, the more alert your subconscious will be in your progress toward results. For future focus video templates, visit my Web site at www.phoenixresorthomes.com. When the videos are available, there will be a custom page you can access for ordering.

Next, we will talk about the written business plan as presented here.

Goal Setting and Business Planning

Achieving goals is about quantum physics. Am I kidding? No. There is a way to achieve your goals and all your desires by just thinking about them in the right way. This belief and concept of the universe and our connection to all in it, and our understanding and use of it, is the way to realizing goals, desires, and dreams. These beliefs come first, before you can quantify your business planning goals. With the belief system in place, you can have whatever you desire.

How many novels, historical perspectives, ninja movies, and self-help programs have talked about meditation, harmony, centering on positive thoughts, and so on? And why is that? It's because some people have transcended their average day environs to discover that once they create harmony within and vibrate that harmony with the universe, and then their wants and desires are attracted to them throughout their careers and their personal lives.

Is it easy to retrain our minds to focus on these concepts and to practice them? Not at all. That's because what our parents told us and what the world has taught us is contrary to harmony. It's common to hear words such as don't, can't, and no from parents, teachers, siblings and friends. They believe they are creating a safe environment for us. However, if you put out these vibes to the universe, what you'll get back is more of what you sent out—negatives. That will lead to generating more negative vibes.

The world, in its ideal state, is balanced. All the atoms, particles, and bits are in perfect balance, and when we align ourselves with this balance, we get balance in return. More importantly, what we desire and what we want can be driven to us by thinking about them in a positive way.

Try this:

Decide what you really want, ignoring the things you don't want. Write it all down. Make a long list if you choose. Be as specific as you can. Use the outline provided in this book if it helps.

Focus on your desires. Every night when you go to bed, picture them as having been achieved. Do this while in perfect balance with all around you-harmony within yourself, quiet, peaceful, and in serene environments... Breathe deeply, softly, and with peace in your mind. Your subconscious will empower you and seek the balance in the universe, attracting to you what you really want and desire. I assure you this works. I've done it for years, and most of my successes have come from knowing exactly what I wanted, when I wanted it. I didn't have to struggle or force it to happen. The subconscious is not an evaluative organ. It seeks to adjust its vibrations to whatever is put there. So be careful what you ask for; you will get it.

Here's an example of how this process worked for me, but you may find it hard to believe: One day I was out driving in the pouring rain, having a great, blissful day—my husband had finally gotten a job, and we were on our way out of debt. I had run an errand, come back to the car with a happy and cheerful spirit, started to drive off, and noticed one of those flyers stuck to my windshield under the wiper. I needed to remove it to see the road. Because I was so in harmony with the universe and because I had no negative thoughts, I simply reached through the windshield, plucked the paper from where it was, and tossed it onto the floorboard. Then it dawned on me I couldn't do that. I reached up to the windshield, and it was solid, but my hand was wet. Did that really happen? Yes. But I knew better than to tell many people—they'd think I had totally lost it. It was quantum physics rearing its head again.

Here's another example: I had earned a bonus at one of the company's I worked for in New York, but the company reneged on paying it. I was in a bad way financially. My mind was whirling about what to do. I was sitting at my desk, thinking about one of our competitors and wishing that I had given more consideration to their past offers, when the phone rang. Guess who it was? The competitor. I knew immediately it was the answer to my situation. They courted me, we made a deal, I took the position that was offered, and the rest is history.

There was also the time I decided to move to Arizona. My husband and I had gone there for our anniversary vacation, and we just loved it. I had been on the East Coast for twenty-nine years, and I decided I could really do without those nasty winters. While we were there, just for grins, we looked at a few lovely homes and talked to the local

Realtor, who was a wealth of information. My vision of living there started to form in my mind, and I also visualized the house model I wanted. The Realtor and I spent some time sharing real estate stories, and he said I should meet the owner of the firm. The next day I did, and within the hour, she offered me a position in Arizona if I wanted to relocate. I got the job, the house, the décor, and I fulfilled the vision I saw. I still live in Arizona and just love it.

The law of attraction works on people, too. All I have to do is think that I wish to hear from my kids and usually within a few minutes, if not immediately, they call. This is kind of nice as I don't have to worry about playing phone tag with them for days. My Mom and I used to call each other every time we had the same dream. Sometimes I would call her as she was dialing me, and we would connect without the phone actually ringing. She's been gone now for a few years, but when I need her wisdom and touch, I only have to think about her and she is with me. She had a good luck symbol—the cardinal. She said that whenever she saw the cardinal, she knew everything would be alright. I see cardinals here whenever I need her touch.

These kinds of connections are very real and can extend to co-workers or business associates, particularly if they are also using the law of attraction or synchronization with the universe. There are all kinds of books out there on how to get yourself to this harmonious place and to realize your dreams, such as *The Secret* by Rhonda Byrne, *Think and Grow Rich* by Napoleon Hill, *As a Man Thinketh* by James Allen, and *Mind over Matter* by Loyd Auerbach.

Business Planning Objectives

Objective (What is it you really want?)

_____

_____

_____

Key Areas of Results:

Who, when, where, how

_____

_____

_____

_____

_____

_____

Action Steps:

Detail of who, when, where, how

_____

_____

_____

_____

_____

_____

_____

_____

_____

_____

_____

_____

Sample-demonstration of the use of the preceding form for goal planning.

Objective:

To generate 3 six month listings over $800,000.00 by November 30, 2009.

Key Areas of Results

- Marketing

  ### Action Steps

  Who: Me, the Web site marketing team

  When: Every Monday afternoon, call for follow up

- Agent Activities

  ### Action Steps

  Who: Me

  Hire admin help in 30 days.

  Create brochure by November 15th

  Create online ad

  Sign up for Craig's List, LinkedIn, FaceBook,

  When: Daily

- Internet development

  Who

  When

  How often

- Video presentations
- CMA presentation

NOTES

Internet Marketing for Real Estate and Sales Professionals

The Changing Paradigm

Eighty-four percent of today's buyers are looking at homes on the Internet. Why else would all the major firms invest so much money and resources in relationships with Trulia, Homes.com, Zillow, Yahoo, FrontDoor, Google, Craigs List, Oodle, and others? It is important for exposing homes for sales and generating buyers.

Internet buyers, on average, take just 2 weeks of your time. Traditional buyers take 6.6 weeks. Internet shopping and selection is faster and easier for today's busy client, no matter what your field. This means less face-to-face time and faster decision making.

It only takes 7.5 showings for an Internet buyer to make a decision to buy, sometimes as little as 2-4. These buyers are savvy; they have done their homework and have been looking and qualifying the homes they want to see. By the time they make their appointment with an agent, they have a good idea of what to pay, where to look, and what price to offer They will usually work with the first agent who calls them back or answers their immediate inquiry. That is why communication is the key to getting clients and their loyalty on the Net. 97 percent agent satisfaction.

The most recent studies from the National Association of Realtors and Realtor.com say that 90 percent of all home buyers and sellers go to the Internet first to research market, mortgage rates, school information, active listings, and general buying/selling information.

The Right Web site Makes a Difference

There are website providers and creators that specialize in real estate sites. The newest kind of website developer such as www.z57.com and www.advancedaccess.com have a format that specifically targets lead generation. There are sites designed for just branding, sites that are designed for featured listings, sites that are company oriented. But, if you want to get actual leads from your site, you need to consult with and use the right developer. It is important to use a website developer that specializes in real estate website development. You want a site that has a customer relationship management system (CRM). It will make a huge difference in your income. Let's say an agent had 10 Internet clients in one year at an average sales price of $290,000, 3 percent coop commission, and 60 percent agent split. That brings a smooth $62,600 per year over and above your usual business. Your CRM should have a built-in automatic follow up system.. This will automatically send out a response to any inquirer who asks for further information from your site. However, because auto responders can vary, you should be able to add your information to them.

Most lead generation Web sites provide a databank—a tracking system—of information: who looked at your site, when, which part of the site did they visit most, did they come back, and so on. These stats are valuable so that the agent has the best chance of contact and conversation of that lead.

Content

Target Audience. Your site should be built for your specific target audience. Your target audience is based on knowing your strengths, your past successes, and your strategic plan.

> Sellers? Buyers? Investors?
>
> Geographic location?
>
> Demographics of each group?
>
> Shopping habits?
>
> Income, Age, Marital Status, Job?

Multiple Listing Service (MLS) Your front page should always have an MLS Search for Homes connection to local MLS. At some point before or during the search, the client should be required to register in several different parts of the site.

Virtual tours. There should be a video presentation of current listings and active listings and have an automatic update when a status changes. This should be sent to buyers and other clients.

Photos. Pictures of current listings should be available whether on the front page as "featured homes" or from the MLS data. The same rules apply as for videos. Most consumers want to see them. The consumers will use the pictures/videos to qualify the home as one to see or not see, so these pictures must be the best.

Informational articles about the market. What is going on in the real estate market today? Are prices going up? What statistics can you share about the neighborhood? MLS can provide these reports. Also, what is going on nationally: bailout, new higher or lower rates?

Neighborhood information: Consumers have personal lives and want to know what the surrounding area can offer them in terms of churches, schools, recreational activities, parks, and so on. Provide this information for them.

School information. What are the scores, ratings, curricula? This is self explanatory, but clients do research this information, so offer them a convenient place to find it.

Entertainment Choices. One of the logical reasons to offer this feature is to keep the clients coming to your site for other valuable information. Offer it for convenience and they will use your site as a center of information.

Home Value information: Free market analysis (CMA). Realtors cannot promise appraisals. Realtors are not licensed appraisers, but most home owners who consider selling will want to get some information on the potential selling price.

Questions and Answers

You can either have a FAQs page with the answers, or you can have a place for buyers/sellers to ask questions and e-mail you.

Helpful buyers/sellers articles. These could be about preparing your home to sell, staging the home to sell, checking for mold, home inspections, and so on.

Unique informational pieces. For example, include a welcome letter, local disclosures documents, local contract forms, agency informational pieces, current market statistics, financing updates, and so on.

Contact Information. This should be prominently displayed throughout the various pages of your site. Be sure to include e-mail addresses and phone and fax numbers.

Handling Internet inquiries. I recommend an auto responder so clients will hear from you right away. I would also call within four hours, preferably sooner if you can. These auto EM responders should contain certain verbiage that will come across as very professional, organized, and prepared. The EM scripts should be what customers expect: short, concise, polite, friendly, interested, thorough, giving the caller something they want, and containing a call to action. The call must be informative and educational and indicate a willingness to help above and beyond what is usual.

Follow-up database system for future business. Each incoming registered inquiry should automatically become entered into a database that you can access in order to design special campaigns by segmenting the buyers/sellers into groups. For example, each time a seller in XYX subdivision registers on your site that EM should automatically pop into a database for that subdivision. This is a great system for generating future business.

How to Make Your Domain Name Work

By Randy Egar.

Randy is a search engine optimization consultant and long-time real estate expert who helps agents get top search engine placement.Ref 12

If a prospect types "Phoenix luxury homes" into a search engine and my Web site domain name is PhoenixLuxuryHomes.com, it is a directly relevant Web site and is given high value in the search engine rankings. This is why having your name or company name as your domain name. may not be a good idea in getting ranked. Why is having your name in your domain name (such as MarySmith.com) *not* good? Because your domain name is one of the first things that the major search engines look at (even before your title) to see how relevant you are to the prospect's search, and one's personal name is not a typical identifying keyword used by the search engines.

Before you say that all the good keyword phrase domain names are gone, you've obviously not included stop words such as my, the, best, site. Of course you know that PhoenixLuxuryHomes.com is taken, but did you know that ThePhoenixLuxuryHomes.com is available for $9.99 a year? Yes, it really is available, as most locations like this are. Also, PhoenixLuxuryHomesSite.com is also available for the same fee. The magic of using these stop words is that the major search engines don't index them, and so they are invisible to the search engines. Thus ThePhoenixLuxuryHomes.com has the same impact as PhoenixLuxuryHomes.com. Want to test it? Just type this search into Google and take a look at the results line that shows how many competing Web sites there are. You'll note that the word **the** is black and not underlined. Thus, it is not a hyperlink. All the other words are.

So all we've learned so far is how to buy valuable domain names. Next, we must understand why we want to do this. The answer should be clear: how many times do you think that someone types your name into their search engine? Only a few will. And that brings me to my main point.

You can and should have your name as your domain name but not for search engines. You should do this for humans. We can remember easily spelled names such as domain names. But how do we combine the use of our domain name that has our personal name (for the human element) with the keyword rich (words search engines will identify as key for the search) domain name (for the search engine element)? It's just three steps:

1. Go to GoDaddy (or any other domain seller) and research and purchase a good keyword rich domain name. A keyword rich domain name has your location and services included.

2. Ask your Internet service provider (or the company that is hosting your Web site) to move it (not copy it) to the new keyword rich domain. They'll know what to do.

3. This step is most important, and the ISP should know how to do it. Tell them to put a 301 redirector on your old website, which will redirect traffic from your old domain with your name to your new domain location. (A 301 redirector is called a permanent redirector and is good for the search engines.) To the viewer, they will know no difference. You will still have the same Web site and it will happen so fast they will not know they are being redirected.

Now what do you have? You have your MarySmith.com domain on your business card for the human element, and yet you are using the better keyword rich domain name for the search engines to find you better. So you are using the best of both worlds.

One final *very important note*—If you already have a high page rank with Google and your domain name is *not* keyword rich, don't do anything. The search engines already know you under your current name. Altering it could be bad.

A second *very important note*—When you buy this new keyword rich domain name, make sure you buy it for ten years. Google gives you extra credit if they know you are not a spammer.

Are Teams Right For You

The Formation of Teams (13)

Adapted Article from RISMEDIA.2007 By Dick Zeller

Dick Zeller is an agent, investor and President & CEO of Real Estate Champions. His company trains more than 250,000 agents worldwide each year through live events, online training, self-study programs, and newsletters. He's the author of Your First Year in Real Estate, Success as a Real Estate Agent for Dummies®, The Champion Real Estate Agent, and over 300 articles in print

RISMEDIA, July 31, 2007–

I see more agents today trying to establish teams in their practices than ever before, . The concept is good, but the planning needs to be complete and thorough and they are trying to create them much earlier in their careers. I even see agents with less than one year in the business that are marginally successful trying to attract others to work with them in that unstable environment.

For too many people, their team building days are premature. Many agents don't have the sales, marketing, leadership, and business skills to find their way out of a wet paper bag but are still trying to create teams. If sales and lead generation are inconsistent, a team will not solve those problems.

If you don't have a powerful administrative assistant, hiring a bunch of inexperienced buyer's agents won't solve the revenue problem. The real truth is it will make the revenue problem worse. The buyer's agents will divert your attention from the revenue-generating activities that you must do. You will end up helping the buyer's agents manage and shepherd their transactions to closing. You will gain a portion of their production but will lose most of yours to do it. That certainly isn't the pathway to becoming a champion team.

The birth of real estate teams really began in the early '90s. Agents looked to leverage themselves through other people who could help them serve their clients better. By removing some of the more repetitive activities of the business that generated little new revenue, the administrative assistant was born. A few years later, successful agents were beginning to expand or leverage themselves by hiring sales assistants on the buyer side of the transaction. These successful lead agents would have buyer's agents (or buyer's specialists) to handle the buyer side of the business, which is more labor intensive.

I hired my first administrative assistant in 1991. I had no idea what I was doing, and neither did she. In those early days, there wasn't a blueprint to follow. Most everyone, including me, learned the hardest way—through trial and error. I messed up a lot but eventually figured it out. I created a mountain of success on top of piles of failure. Fortunately, you won't have to learn that way. You can be the beneficiary of my experience to vastly lower your mistakes.

Before you dive into birthing your new team, I really believe you have to answer some key questions about yourself and your business.(6)

1. Am I really prepared to lead people?

2. Do I have enough leads to support a team?

3. What size of team do I see five years from now?

4. What sales volume do I expect in five years?

5. Am I willing to increase my prospecting now?

The "PROS" of a team

The positives are easy to spot for most agents who are considering expanding their business through a team. It's easy to put on the rose colored glasses to evaluate the possibility of establishing a team.

The positives are certainly that you will have more people working to service your clients and prospects . . . even if you are just adding an administrative assistant. Your level of service with a well trained, professional administrative assistant is higher than a singular agent can provide. All of the administrative functions such as feedback from agent showings, sending copies of advertisements to sellers, and creating marketing flyers and brochures can be done quicker, better, and more efficiently through an assistant than by a single agent.

Certainly, you will also be able to achieve greater balance between your business and family time by leveraging yourself through a team. Being able to have weekends off for your family is a large benefit in my view. I truly believe my effectiveness as a salesperson and business owner was enhanced because I didn't work Friday, Saturday, or Sunday—as most agents did. It allowed me to be "on vacation" each weekend to enjoy the fruits of my labor with my wife, Joan. It would be even more important for me today with children to raise and enjoy.

As the lead agent, you will have a larger amount of time to invest in Direct Income Producing Activities (DIPA). That's where most lead agents who are building teams fall off the path to success. They fail to increase their DIPA time to increase their revenue.

With a team, you gain the ability to delegate what I view as the worst segment of real estate sales, which is dealing with the emotional roller coaster ride that clients often take you on. The roller coaster of emotion can last through the entire listing process and includes hand holding, extra service, and the high expectations of many clients. These clients are often on the razor's edge of emotion. We need to service them well, but often, their worst fears and problems can set even the most seasoned, experienced agent into an activity funk. When you achieve a sale, you can often start back up the roller coaster again. Having a skilled team can protect you from these emotional swings, peaks, and valleys. A great team or great assistant can help protect you from a client's challenges that could wipe you out and keep you from revenue producing activities for a few days.

One trait of a Champion Lead Agent is their ability to avoid being taken off the track toward their goals. The arrows of running a service-based business don't cause them to go down for the rest of the week or day. The mark of a Champion is someone who, when they go off track, doesn't allow that time of frustration or lack of focus and intensity to be more than a few minutes, rather than hours, days, or weeks.

The "CONS" of a team

The biggest con of a team is the inevitable trial and error that change creates. Even with a complete blueprint to success, errors will occur. Change is a constant.

There are certainly cons that are created through hiring more people. The management, motivation, and coaching of staff is a blessing and a curse. There is nothing more gratifying in life than assisting and guiding people in growth. There is nothing more frustrating in life than assisting and guiding people in growth. The management challenges grow exponentially with each person you add to the team. Your skills as the leader, coach, and motivator need to grow, as well.

If you hire talented people, your biggest challenge will be staying ahead of them in terms of your learning and skills. The most challenging aspect of my job is staying ahead of my staff, my clients, my coaches, and the real estate industry. It takes a tremendous expenditure of time, emotion, and energy to accomplish that.

Near Mistakes I Made and the Lessons I Learned

I did really quite well during my real estate management career by learning how to function in a man's world, having terrific mentors, and learning from some near misses.

Example 1

After doing very well with the very first office I managed, I was promoted to an office within a high-end market segment that had numerous high-end producers. The president of the company specifically asked me to take over   this office because it was not doing well. He wanted this office turned around quickly. I thought I could do it, so I agreed and took over. The orders of the commander were this: make this office a winner; do whatever it takes. Even though I had a mentor relationship with the president of the company, I still had to prove myself. Based on my recent history, great things were expected.

The very first thing that the agents complained about was that the facility itself didn't measure up for a high-end market. Indeed, this was true. It was on the shabby, dark side and was just tired looking. The ceilings were low, the carpet was dingy, the light was limited, and the desks were plain worn out. Just about this time, the national convention was held in Hawaii, and I was expected to go, so I did. And I had a great time. I don't think I made it to a single meeting, but I did check in for the registration, so everyone assumed I was there on site. One of the couples I partied down with was the rehab manager for a competing firm in our high-end market. He and I made a deal, and when we returned home, he came over and started rehabbing. I ordered reception furniture from one of our office catalogs and got old, solid wood desks out of storage. Things were looking up. The agents were excited.

Now keep in mind, I did have a regional manager—let's call him Bob. Although I was a chosen manager, I did have a direct supervisor other than the president, and unfortunately, he was one of the most conservative, constrained, serious managers I have ever worked with. Well, Bob decided to visit our office one Saturday, and he happened to come in during the rehab, which he did not know about. Actually, I didn't share this information with anyone, being unaware that most of what I was doing required other approvals and budget considerations. After all, my directive had been "do whatever it takes." And I was doing just that.

Well, Bob took one look around and almost had a stroke on the spot. He showed up in my office first thing Monday morning and asked me what I thought I was doing. I explained to him it was all covered—the president had asked me to do whatever it took to turn the office around. He was red in the face, stuttering, and generally extremely upset. I was in his region, and he hadn't planned this. I carefully went through the plan and the very reasonable costs, but it didn't seem to appease him much. I told him maybe he should check in with John, the president of the company. So Bob left. Within an hour, I got a call from John, calmly explaining to me, with some humor, that what I had done required a couple of approvals and a budget approval to boot. I said it was a little late to decide because new carpet was being laid and we needed drywall and paint, not to mention a door for a new section I had opened up. He then said he would take care of it all and I should continue to do what I was doing. He admired my determination and spunk and said he would smooth it over with Bob. I got the bills off to the CFO, and we all lived happily ever after. The office went on to improve production by over 100 percent, and I was promised by John—my mentor, my friend, and my boss—that when a regional position was available, it would be mine. There's some truth to the saying, "Do what you must and ask for forgiveness later." But this was not the end for me and Bob or even me and John.

Example 2

John was so pleased with the results in the upper-end market that he decided that I should also work with select managers who were having less success than was needed. I was to continue running my own office, too, but because it was doing very well, I was allowed to help the others. In addition, since I knew I was going to be a regional manager within the year, I chose my successor and started training him. There was one catch: Bob was still my regional supervisor, and my plans had to go through him first. He fought me on every change or suggestion I recommended. In the meantime, John had hired a VP named Jim. So I was to work with Bob and Jim, and I was given the title Assistant Regional Manager. None of this was taken well by Bob. Jim was an odd dude: very quiet and quixotic. Since John liked me and supported me, Jim leaned that way, too. But he also supported and respected Bob.

The stonewalling from Bob continued, and I became even more frustrated, partly because I was not having the success with the other offices I thought I could if given free rein, and partly because getting any plans approved by Bob was both exhausting and time consuming. So one day when I was in HQ for a meeting, I asked Jim if he had a minute. This line of command was established corporate protocol now, and I had somewhat limited access to John. That's how it goes sometimes. I told Jim about Bob blocking my every change or plan and that if things were to improve for the failing offices,I needed more cooperation from Bob. Jim was most gracious and said he'd talk to Bob. Well, he did, and Bob became even more thwarting and difficult.

Needless to say, the failing offices were clamoring for more and more attention, and I was trying desperately to help but having more and more difficulty getting it done. The next time I was in HQ, this was maybe two months after my first discussion with Jim, I saw him in the cafeteria and asked if I could join him. He agreed, and we sat down to chat. I finally got to my complaint about Bob, again, and told Jim all about it. Then I got the first part of my lesson. He said, "Laura, I am sorry to hear that." Whereupon he said not another word and got up and left me sitting there.

I went to my car. It was very hot, and I had the air conditioning running, and I sat there and thought, "What did he mean by saying that? Why was he being so vague?" Then I got it. If I were to be a successful leader, it was up to me to solve the problem, not keep going to him or John to fix things for me. I had to fix this problem all by myself. It was a test.

On returning to the office, I mentally sketched out a plan. I called Bob and asked for him to come by the office for a short visit. He was a bit surprised to hear from me, but he willingly came out. Once he was there, I went through an explanation that our working together was a test for both of us. It was a test for me to see if I was truly leadership material, and it was a test for him to see if he could handle new creative, innovative leaders and out of the box thinking. He stared at me for some time and then said in a quiet voice, "Holy cow, I do believe you are right." We agreed that we should become each other's best friend and supporter and vocalize this often to our superiors. If we were to do this, we would both come out heroes and winners. So that's what he and I did, and in addition, we became friends and went on to have many good successes together. Our leaders were proud of us and happy about the new working relationship we had. Everyone won. It served me well to learn this very important and valuable lesson early on in my career. Leadership means seeking within one's self and understanding the truth of a situation, and then doing something about it to solve it. You cannot depend on someone else to solve your problems.

Example 3

Let us continue with this same national firm for one more lesson— one hard learned and never to be forgotten. As you know, John, the president of this firm, and I were friends as well as associates. He had depended on me, and I had come through for him. He was appreciative and impressed. He promised me a regional position when the next one was available. Well, one year later John was promoted to run all the Eastern offices for this national firm, so he left my firm and the area and ended up in New Jersey. He was replaced with another man who also was an acquaintance and later friend, but he was not of John's imagination or ability. Our firm had acquired another large local firm and merged them into our company, which meant many management jobs were taken or created for them. Guess what? My regional job had gone to someone else from there. I called Fred, the new president, and asked about it. He said, "Yes, I know that John had picked you for the next regional position, but we now have this acquisition, and we had to place their leaders in the leadership positions. There's no regional position available for our own people. I'm sorry, but that's the way it is." Well, here I was, ready to move up, and I was struck by the law of happenstance. What was I to do? I had my replacement and had positioned my office for the transition, and now I had no where to go. Or did I?

I picked up the phone and called John in New Jersey. He was glad to hear from me. We agreed to meet. On a Saturday, I drove up to New Jersey and spent some time chatting about my future. He said I could have a regional job, either in New York or New Jersey, which one did I want? I asked his opinion, and he said "Well, you know the old adage, 'If you can succeed in New York, you can succeed anywhere.' I'd take New York." So I did. I was divorced at the time, so life was a bit of a mess for me, but I never looked back. I resigned from my current position, sold my house to my new manager, and headed for New York. I found a house there under construction and bought it with the help of the company, and I went into my first important regional position. It was a challenge, for sure, but when a door opens, there's a reason, and you should walk through it. Sometimes adversity can lead to opportunities.

Example 4

The regional job in New York developed nicely. When I was hired, I was on a compensation grid as a bonus, and it was based on production as well as time. If one achieved the desired production within the time frame, the highest bonus was available. In this case, it was $17,000.00. I met the test—again—and was due this bonus in my next check. It wasn't there. I had a supervisor in New York, but he wasn't defined as the president of the firm. He may have been designated as a SVP or COO, but he was not called president. His name was Bill. When I didn't get my check, I asked Bill about it. He said he'd check on it. The next month, the check didn't come, or the next month. Finally, I went in late one afternoon and asked if I was ever going to get the bonus. I was depending on it as the move and finishing the house I bought had cost me plenty, and I had taken a pay cut just to have the regional position. He said, "Not really. We didn't think you could really achieve it in the first place, so we didn't budget for it. I'm sorry, but we just don't have the budget to pay you the bonus." This was not good and definitely not what I wanted to hear. I was stunned. I went to my office and stared out the window. It was raining and already depressing. I was thinking, "What have I done? How am I going to make it now? I need a solution." And, lo and behold, the phone rang. It was one of the leaders of a highly respected national competitor. He was located in the city where I had formerly worked and knew me and my reputation. He had also been promoted, so he was in charge of the eastern seaboard of offices for his firm, and he was CEO/President of this huge firm. We had a nice chat, and he asked if I would meet with him next time I came south to his area. I said I'd be delighted, and he said he might have an interesting proposal for me.

About three weeks later, on a Saturday, we met in his office. I was actually on the way to the beach on a short vacation with my new beau. The executive and I must have talked for three hours. He asked me how I liked New York, and I told him that I liked it very well but I was not making enough money to exist there. He asked me if I'd like to triple my income and responsibility. I said I would. He then told me of the position he was about to create—president of the New York firm. He was in the process of restructuring the tristate firms and wanted me to run New York. He had some positioning to do, and it took about thirty days to complete, but then I was named the new president of the New York division of this huge, nationally ranked firm. I did not call John to tell him I was leaving. He was very upset when he found out. Some three months later, he called me at home one weekend and said, "You broke my heart. Why did you really leave?" I told him the truth: I had worked hard to do the job, and the firm had reneged on what they promised—to pay my well-earned bonus. He said he never knew about it and asked why I hadn't called him. I told him I had learned to figure out my own problems and solve them, and that didn't include whining or complaining to management.

The next two and a half years were dizzying. I had all kinds of new challenges and even had to totally restructure the New York firm. I chose one of my female colleagues to help me. She has gone on to head up one of the largest, most successful firms in the nation. I am very proud of her considerable achievements. We are still best friends.

I got married and was brought back to my home area, Maryland/DC/Virginia, where I joined with four other leaders of the large national firm I led in New York. We formed a partnership when our national entity was sold to an even larger national entity. It was a five-state franchise that was highly successful and attained a highly respected status among national firms. Eight years later, in one of the disastrous real estate recessions, we were forced to sell. But all the people and all the lessons learned during these twenty years were most enlightening. I'm pleased to have shared them with you.

When I hear other real estate professionals whine and complain, I think about the adversities my new husband and I overcame both personally and professionally. During the above time periods, I had a massive, but nonmalignant, brain tumor; a stroke; and a hip replacement. The man I married had throat and neck cancer, a brain tumor (also nonmalignant), prostate cancer, a hip replacement, and triple bypass surgery. In business, I was partner in a 5 state firm that did an outstanding 7 B a year production. This firm was sold in 1996. Then, I went back to school and got a Masters Degree in information technology management. I opened and was successful for 7 years with a small boutique brokerage using the knowledge I had learned from the new degree. Next, I worked with the largest mega broker on the Eastern seaboard, and opened a million dollar office. Next, we sold everything and moved to Arizona. Amazingly, after twenty years together, we are both fine and still kickin' and still working.

Remember we all have to start somewhere and take the challenge I will never forget my very first strategic planning event as a brand new manager. A three-day meeting was held outside of corporate so that we could all focus on delivering a valid projection of the next six month's office production. All us managers—thirteen men and three women—were supposed to bring their budget plans, but since I was just hired, I had no idea what to submit or how it was to be prepared. My SVP, my boss, assured me he "had it covered for me." The CEO was a sort of no-nonsense kind of guy and went around to each manager asking for their projected numbers. I was so afraid of making a bad impression, afraid that the SVP would give out incorrect numbers, afraid of being embarrassed, and afraid of not knowing what I should say, that I hyperventilated and passed out cold in the adjacent hallway while trying to escape to the lady's room for a brief getting-it-together respite. Well, I definitely did make an impression on all present. Frankly, I think they were all rather amused that I was so nervous that I fainted, and they cut me some slack for the next two days. It was the only time in my career I ever went into a budget meeting not fully prepared. I did hyperventilate a few times, but with knowledge, I outgrew it.

Well, that wraps it up for this episode. I will be writing more books about leadership, management, and real estate. I hope you enjoy this one enough to look for the new books as they come out. You can always find them at www.lulu.com and www.phoenixresorthomes.com.

See you next time! Lana

Bibliography

1. The Secret by Rhonda Byrne,

   Think and Grow Rich by Napoleon Hill,

   As a Man Thinketh by James Allen,

   Mind over Matter by Loyd Auerbach.

2. The Speed of Trust: The One Thing that Changes Everything. Stephen Covey

3. The Effective Executive, Peter Drucker

4. Personal Coaching for Results, Lou Tice

5. The Invisible Force, Dr. Wayne Dwyer and.Change Your Thoughts, Dr. Wayne Dwyer

6. The Seven Habits of Highly Effective People, Stephen Covey

7. A Passion for Excellence Tom Peters and Nancy Austin

8. The Effective Executive, Peter Drucker

9. Liberation Management: Necessary Disorganization for the Nanosecond Nineties, Peter Drucker

10. A Passion for Excellence, Tom Peters

11. The One Minute Manager, Kenneth Blanchard and Spencer Johnson

Lana Cloud, a veteran professional and top management executive of over thirty years, is the president and broker of Kache' Realty Group, LLC, a firm that personifies the new advanced-technology paradigms in the sales industry since the recent economic crisis—personalized, comprehensive services both online and in person.

Lana obtained her first sales license in New Mexico in 1974. She obtained her broker license and her first management position in real estate in 1982.

Since then, she has led single offices, groups of offices, and regional divisions for a number of national leaders including Coldwell Banker, Merrill Lynch, Prudential Preferred Properties, and Weichert Realtors. Her particular field of expertise is in rebuilding and growing real estate offices, divisions, or firms that need organizational and developmental leadership. She also coaches associates to their highest and best performances.

Lana was the president of Merrill Lynch Realty, New York, from 1987 to 1990 and an owner of Prudential Preferred Properties on the East Coast from 1990 to 1995. Prudential was a five-state franchise with sixty-nine offices and over four billion dollars in annual revenues. The firm was sold in 1995, and Cloud then ran her own E realty firm—a small, upscale, boutique brokerage—from 1995 to 2003.

Cloud's expertise is diversified, and her contributions to all aspects of real estate and sales organizations have been valuable to the firms and associates she has coached. She now endeavors to give back to her industry and to the hundreds of mentors and clients who have been instrumental in her success through her firm, Kache Realty Group,LLC and its outstanding services.

www.ingramcontent.com/pod-product-compliance
Lightning Source LLC
Chambersburg PA
CBHW021041180526
45163CB00005B/2232